Bodybu

small group bible resources

Surviving under pressure

finding strength in the tough times

Christopher Griffiths
& Stephen Hathway

Scripture Union, 207–209 Queensway, Bletchley, MK2 2EB, England.
Email:info@scriptureunion.org.uk
www.scriptureunion.org.uk

Scripture Union Australia, Locked Bag 2, Central Coast Business Centre, NSW 2252

Small Group Resources, 1 Hilton Place, Harehills, Leeds, LS8 4HE

Note: *Surviving Under Pressure* was originally published under the title *Don't Give In*.

ISBN 1 85999 587 X

Scripture quotations are taken from the Holy Bible, New International Version. Copyright
© 1973, 1978, 1984 by International Bible Society. Anglicisation copyright © 1979, 1984, 1989.
Used by permission of Hodder and Stoughton Ltd.

British Library Cataloguing-in-Publication Data
A catalogue record for this book is available from the British Library.

Cover design by David Lund Design
Internal page design by David Lund Design
Internal page layout by Mac Style Ltd, Scarborough, N. Yorkshire

Printed and bound in Great Britain by Ebenezer Baylis & Son Ltd, The Trinity Press, London
Road, Worcester WR5 2JH

Introducing Bodybuilders

 ## ORIGINS AND APPROACH

BODYBUILDERS resources have a strong emphasis on building relationships, helping groups discover the real meaning of **koinonia** – the loving fellowship of Christian believers within which people really care for one another. Group members are encouraged to apply God's Word in ways that produce action and change – all within a secure, supportive atmosphere.

This relational approach to small group experience was first developed in the US by author Lyman Coleman under the title *Serendipity*. In the 1980s Scripture Union, in partnership with another publisher, *Small Group Resources*, took that as the foundation of nine studies under the *Serendipity* branding specially written for the UK market.

This **BODYBUILDERS** series recognises the value and strength of the *Serendipity* approach and contains much of the original material. In a sense, homegroups of the early 21st century may be far more ready to adopt this relational approach than their predecessors. Home groups have moved on; expectations have changed. Revisions and extra new material reflect that progress and also make the series pioneering in the sense of providing a more complete off-the-shelf package.

Christians are not immune from the pressures of society – stresses in the home, workplace, college, places of social interaction. When questioned, most people admit to a deep need for security, a sense of belonging, and a safe environment in which to share themselves and be given support. Many are dissatisfied with the superficial relationships that often characterise contemporary living. They identify lonely chasms in their inner beings, empty of meaningful relationships. They long for practical ways in which to work out their heart commitment to Jesus Christ.

Central to the approach is an understanding that satisfying relationships can be nurtured in small groups in dynamic ways when people are prepared to take risks in opening themselves up to God and to each other. This shared vulnerability works within four contexts:

- **storytelling**
- **affirmation**
- **goal setting**
- **koinonia**

People need to share themselves and need to hear others sharing their own lives for relationships to grow. This is **storytelling**. Everyone needs to be listened to. When we respond to someone with a 'thank you', or 'I found your contribution helpful', we demonstrate that they are valuable and have a contribution to make to the growth of others. This is **affirmation**. Experiencing this in a group that meets regularly – even over a limited time – people begin to share their deeper longings or hurts, discovering that they can trust others for support in their struggles. Individuals can listen for what God is saying to them and implement

3

changes – **goal setting** within the security of **koinonia**. **BODYBUILDERS** encourage all these stages to be reached through Bible study.

MEETING NEEDS IN CHURCHES AND COMMUNITIES

BODYBUILDERS aim to meet:

* **the need for applied biblical knowledge** – Christians are crying out for help in applying their faith in a confusingly complex world. Knowing what the Bible says isn't enough; people want to know how to translate knowledge into action.
* **the need to belong** – increasing pressures, accelerating pace of life, constant change: these work against committed relationships, which many feel should be a distinctive feature of the local church as it witnesses to a lonely generation.
* **the need to share the burden** – pressures on Christians are often intolerable, as demonstrated by emotional/ psychological disorders, increasing divorce rates, and the problems of ineffective parenting. One answer is for Christians to take seriously the sharing of each others' burdens – not only prayerfully but practically.
* **the need to build the church as community** – there is a growing conviction that the church should be a community living out the true nature of God's kingdom, experiencing New Testament koinonia.

BODYBUILDERS IN PRACTICE

Using BODYBUILDERS to form new groups: The ideal size for a group is between five and 12, meeting in a home or a church. Newcomers can be added into the group at any time, but care should be taken to give them a thorough briefing on 'the story so far'. The particular purposes of the group in growing relationships and discovering how to apply Bible truths to everyday life need to be made plain.

Using BODYBUILDERS in established groups: This material differs from much on the market to resource small groups. Make sure from the outset that the group appreciates that it is more interactive and, in some ways, more demanding. There is an emphasis on application as well as understanding.

Leading the BODYBUILDERS Group: If belonging to this group can be demanding, leading it is more so! The leader needs to have thought about the **BODYBUILDERS** approach and the goals. Ideally, there needs to be knowledge of the group, too, so that the material can be adapted to meet their particular needs. Options are given, and it is the leader who decides which and how much of that material is appropriate. Bearing in mind the emphasis on relationship building, the leader must ensure the group does not become a 'clique', too inward-looking or isolated. The leader makes sure everyone has a chance to speak, assisting those who find contributing difficult. He or she may need to take the initiative in promoting relationship building, which might include practical things like providing lists of telephone numbers, encouraging lift sharing, even organising a baby-sitting rota, as well as exercising pastoral care and leadership.

Each group member needs to feel committed to building relationships and willing to share personally. Regular attendance is a priority. Members aim to make themselves available to each other. Make sure everyone knows that there is complete confidentiality in respect of all that is shared. Encourage prayer for each other between meetings – and set an example yourself.

Practically speaking, you will need plenty of pens and large sheets of plain paper, and sometimes supplies of felt-tip pens, scissors, glue and old magazines or newspapers. Some Icebreakers need pre-prepared visual aids, or even some re-arrangement of furniture! Look ahead to plan for the coming sessions.

All the booklets in this series, each self-contained, contain material for six sessions. Some groups may want to add an introductory evening to explain the **BODYBUILDERS** approach, perhaps in a social setting over a pot-luck meal. The material can be worked through at a slower pace, if that is preferred.

Most of the interactive material is confined to a double-page spread for each session, so that the leader can photocopy it as an A4 sheet to be given out. Alternatively, everyone can have their own copy of the book. Make sure you allow people enough time to jot down answers on their response sheets. Ring the changes: sometimes it's helpful for people to complete responses in twos or threes, especially when a little discussion time is appropriate.

Variety and freedom are hallmarks of the **BODYBUILDERS** material. Leaders can select from the material to put together each session's programme:

Prayer/ Worship (variable time) – options are given, so that you can tailor your selection to whatever your group feels most comfortable with. Hymns and songs suggested are drawn from several popular collections currently on the market published by Kingsway: various

editions *of Songs and Hymns of Fellowship, Spring Harvest Praise, New Songs* and *Stoneleigh* and *The Source*. Your group may be more comfortable with songs from other traditions. It is always helpful, though, to try to match songs to the theme.

Icebreaker (15 minutes) – this warm-up session is intended to relax the group and focus them on being together, and is usually based on the theme.

Relational Bible study (15 minutes) – this is an initial, fairly light excursion into the Bible verses, relating them to the lives of those in the group through multiple choice questions. If the group is large or time is limited, it may be that not everyone shares every question. By the way, Bible verses quoted in **BODYBUILDERS** almost always come from the NIV (New International Version), but you can use another translation. Often it's helpful to have a selection of different translations to compare when studying a particular passage.

In Depth (20 minutes) – moving deeper into the Bible verses, discovering more about their relationship to life.

My story (10–20 minutes) – an encouragement for people to relate teaching to everyday lives.

Going further (15 minutes) – this often involves other parts of the Bible containing similar teaching. If not used during group time, this can be taken away for further personal study during the week.

Enjoy! Discover! Grow!

BODYBUILDERS
small group Bible resources

Relationship Building – growing a caring and committed community
Lance Pierson

It's impossible to live daily life without constant interaction with the people around us: family, neighbours, friends or workmates. These six sessions will help you and your group develop the skills needed to build healthy relationships.
ISBN 1 85999 582 9

Designed for great things – wrestling with human nature
Anton Baumohl

Human beings – beautiful and unique yet rebellious and capable of evil! Only the Christian view of man makes real sense of the good and bad things about being human. These six sessions will help you and your group to discover your true potential in Christ.
ISBN 1 85999 585 3

Living for the King – growing God's rule in our world
'Tricia Williams

'God in control? It doesn't look like it!' Is that your reaction to the suffering and injustice you see in the world? These six sessions look at key issues which have immediate relevance for those who want to be involved in the risky and exciting business of being God's community here and now.
ISBN 1 85999 584 5

Growing through change – seizing the opportunities life gives you
Lance Pierson

Do we fear change because we have mis-placed our emotional security? These six sessions challenge you and your group to find security in God himself, to welcome any kind of change as an opportunity to deepen that trust, and to discover strength and support in the community of the church.
ISBN 1 85999 585 7

A Fresh Encounter – meeting the real Jesus
David Bolster

Some were intrigued, attracted to him, accepted, loved and followed him; others were afraid of him, were disturbed by him or rejected him. These six sessions challenge you and your group to extend your understanding of who Jesus is and what that means in everyday life.
ISBN 1 85999 586 1

Available from all good Christian bookshops or from Scripture Union Mail Order:
PO Box 5148, Milton Keynes MLO, MK2 2YX, Tel: 01908 856006
or online through www.scriptureunion.org.uk

SURVIVING UNDER PRESSURE
– finding strength in the tough times

INTRO

Following Christ in the twenty-first century isn't easy. We live high-pressure lives, bombarded with conflicting views and influences that can become real obstacles to adopting a lifestyle that truly reflects Christian values and principles. Each of us has experienced – and maybe continues to experience – times when we've been struggling, when our faith has been stretched to the limits.

Jesus never claimed that living as a member of his kingdom would be easy or problem-free. In fact, he prepared his would-be followers by warning them of opposition ahead.

Peter, one of the leaders of the early church, had the tremendous experience of sharing part of his life with Jesus. He spent time on the road with Jesus, he listened daily to his teaching, he watched as he performed miracles, he witnessed his resurrection. Throughout it all, he knew the struggles and hardships of being a follower of Christ. Who better, then, to help us as we work through out own difficulties?

Peter wrote a letter to fellow believers scattered throughout Asia Minor (Turkey) in which he encouraged them in their struggles. This letter, which we know as 1 Peter, recognises the cost of living in what is in effect an alien world, a world where there are many obstacles to living as a Christian – a world we can identify with today.

Peter's letter offers us help, inspiration and hope. He points his readers forward to a time when they will live in God's presence, but understands that the journey may sometimes be on rough ground. We are encouraged to be faithful to Christ despite all the problems, to live in a way which is worthy of Jesus, and to work to become a caring community which not only offers worship to God but serves and supports one another through good and bad times.

STAND FIRM!

AIM: To see that times of testing are a normal part of Christian life.

NOTES FOR LEADERS

It will be important to establish an atmosphere of warmth and trust in which people are encouraged to contribute and know that they will be valued for any contribution they make. Spend a few minutes giving an overview of the subjects to be covered, and make sure that everyone knows the number of meetings and venues.

PRAYER/WORSHIP IDEAS

Opening prayer

Set a relaxed and warm tone as you commit everyone's varying expectations to God and ask for growth in understanding, in personal commitment, in relationships.

Worship

As this is a first meeting for the group, encourage everyone to be free to express themselves in worship in ways they find meaningful, and to be accepting of the way others may choose to worship. Make clear that clapping or raising hands or arms etc are acceptable (indeed, biblical!), as are different postures for prayer (kneeling, sitting, standing etc).

Throughout the six meetings it would be helpful to choose hymns or songs which focus on God as our source of strength, security and hope, as well as those which reflect truths particularly relevant to the weekly studies. For this opening meeting some suggestions are:

Father, I place into your hands
For the joys and for the sorrows
Hail to the Lord's anointed
He is our peace
How sweet the name of Jesus sounds
I give you all the honour
Jesus, you are changing me
O worship the Lord in the beauty of holiness
Praise my soul, the King of heaven
When we walk with the Lord

During the meeting

Give everyone an A4 sheet on which to draw the outline of a range of mountains. Invite them to label each one briefly with an area of struggle or pressure which they feel is inhibiting their relationship with God. Encourage them to be specific, labelling their mountains with things like, 'Bad relationship with Sarah at the office', 'Too tired to pray when I should', 'Feel discouraged about debt', 'As a dad I don't manage to spend enough time with the kids'. Choose one mountain to pray about with a partner.

Closing prayer

As leader, pick up on any concerns about struggles that have come up during the meeting, particularly those mentioned in the My Story slot.

ICEBREAKER

In pairs, everyone recalls one experience of testing to share with a partner. This could be something like school or college exams, driving test, sports competitions, demanding job interviews etc. When each has shared an event, ask everyone to talk with their partner about the way that particular event affected their life, negatively or positively, or both. For example, failing a driving test might have meant not being able to apply for a particular promotion; running a marathon might have meant a picture in the local paper and the invitation to speak to a youth group. If there's time, you might want to encourage some sharing with the whole group.

BIBLE READING
I Peter 1:3–9

RELATIONAL BIBLE STUDY
If the group is large, sharing might be better in pairs, threes or fours.

IN DEPTH

MY STORY

GOING FURTHER
If you do this during the group meeting, give everyone a different passage to investigate. After five to ten minutes of individual study, encourage people to share their discoveries.

Things to remember ...

---

notes on the Bible verses

 I Peter 1:3–9

Peter probably wrote this letter from Rome during a time when the believers in Jesus were scattered and being persecuted by the Roman authorities.

1:3 The resurrection of Christ was the central theme of early Christian preaching and here Peter links it with the Christian's hope. You might want to refer to part of Peter's sermon on the Day of Pentecost (Acts 2:25) or Paul's teaching on the resurrection in I Corinthians 15.

1:4 The Old Testament focuses on the deliverance of God's people from slavery in Egypt to their inheritance of the Promised Land

of Canaan. Here Christian salvation is thought of in terms of deliverance from sin into fellowship with God.

1:6,7 Peter encourages faithfulness, saying that trials are to faith what a refining fire is to gold.

1:9 Salvation may be seen in three dimensions:

- **past** – we have been saved, bought with the blood of Christ (Ephesians 2:4,5,8; I Corinthians 6:19,20).
- **present** – we are in the process of being saved, becoming more like Jesus (2 Corinthians 2:15; 3:18).
- **future** – we will be saved, changed to be like Christ when we see him (2 Timothy 4:18; 2 Corinthians 5:1–5; I Corinthians 15:50–55).

STAND FIRM!

BIBLE READING
I Peter 1:3–9

RELATIONAL BIBLE STUDY
Work through the questions on your own, then share your answers with the group.

I What do you think Peter means by *an inheritance … kept in heaven* (1:4)?

_____

2 From this passage, how do you think Peter sees the Christian life? Circle the most appropriate.

a always an uphill struggle

b a bed of roses

c non-stop joy

d white water rafting

e like being a Martian – everyone thinks you're odd

f a nice rosy dream that doesn't really work

g following Jesus whatever happens

h other _____

3 Problems, difficulties, times of stress are… (tick those that are appropriate)

a always the end result of disobeying God.

b meant to teach us something.

c aimed at making life as difficult as possible.

d designed to make faith stronger.

e only experienced by famous Christians.

f what being a Christian's all about.

g other _____

4 To help us get through times of testing we must accept the help that Jesus offers us, and develop a deep relationship with him. The basis of that relationship with Jesus is…

a fear.

b love.

c what the minister says.

d faith.

e being a church member.

f behaving like other Christians.

g watching religious programmes on TV.

h other _____

5 If we endure testing we will…

a be promoted to a kind of super-Christian.

b be praised by Jesus.

c discover everlasting joy.

d be sure of a warm welcome in heaven.

e become a stronger Christian.

f look a bit scorched at the edges.

g become very rich.

h other _____

IN DEPTH

Work through the questions on your own, and then share with the whole group.

I What do you think motivated the early Christians to suffer for their faith?

_____

2 What do you think Peter meant by a *genuine* faith (1:7)?

_____

3 Peter speaks of Christians experiencing *all kinds of trials* (1:6). List ways in which our faith might be tested today.

1 _____   4 _____

2 _____   5 _____

3 _____

MY STORY

1 When my faith is tested I usually ... (put a cross on the line between the two extremes)

give up _____ hang in there

question God _____ trust God

need some help from friends _____ manage on my own

2 In my Christian life I have experienced testing through ... (circle any that apply)

a questions about my faith.   **e** persecution.

b my own stupid mistakes.   **f** problems with relationships.

c physical pain.   **g** being disobedient to God.

d emotional stresses.   **h** other _____

3 In times of testing God will provide help. Check that out in 1 Corinthians 10:13. Here are some of the ways he might choose to give us help. How valuable have you found them? (1= not at all valuable; 10= extremely valuable.)

praying	1	2	3	4	5	6	7	8	9	10
being part of a caring small group	1	2	3	4	5	6	7	8	9	10
reading the Bible	1	2	3	4	5	6	7	8	9	10
reading a Christian book	1	2	3	4	5	6	7	8	9	10
chatting to a friend	1	2	3	4	5	6	7	8	9	10
taking a long walk on my own	1	2	3	4	5	6	7	8	9	10
getting professional help (eg counselling)	1	2	3	4	5	6	7	8	9	10

going further

1 Read Hebrews 4:14–16 and Mark 8:31–33. In what ways was Jesus tested and how did he deal with those situations?

2 Read 2 Corinthians 6:3–10. Paul experienced many times of testing. What enabled him to remain faithful? How can we do the same today? Other

references that would be useful to check out are:
Ephesians 1:17–21; 6:10–20
Philippians 4:10–13
Colossians 1:9–12
2 Timothy: 1:8–12; 3:10–17

CHRIST-LIKE LIVING

AIM: To see that being a Christian disciple means following a Christ-like lifestyle.

NOTES FOR LEADERS

PRAYER/WORSHIP IDEAS

Opening prayer
Spend a few minutes as a group thanking God for sending Jesus to earth and for the example he set for us in every area of his life and ministry.

Songs and hymns
Anything that focuses on Jesus at work in us would be useful during worship. Some ideas include:

Cause me to come to thy river
Change my heart, O God
Jesus, take me as I am
Let there by love shared among us
Lord Jesus, we enthrone you
May the mind of Christ my Saviour
Purify my heart, let me be as gold
Rejoice! Rejoice! Christ is in you
Take my life and let it be
When I look into your holiness

During the meeting
Pray for the gift of Christ's love to share with others, especially with those we find difficult.

Closing prayer
Get everyone to draw two large boxes on a sheet of A4 paper. In one box everyone should draw or list some of the things they or their family own that are valued or especially appreciate, eg 'new widescreen TV', 'watch Dave gave me for Christmas', 'framed photo of Bev on her wedding day',

'my reliable old chest freezer'. In the other box everyone should list some of the things they do that God might value or especially appreciate, eg 'volunteering to clean up after the youth event last Saturday', 'spending 20 minutes reading my Bible and praying yesterday morning', 'biting my tongue when I really wanted to be angry with Steve last night', 'talking to Sheila about God being able to answer prayer hen I bumped into her at the library'. Share and pray in pairs, thanking God for materially blessing each other; ask him to be at work in each other's lives, increasing their fruitfulness for the kingdom.

ICEBREAKER
This exercise asks the group to use everyday things to describe their lives, which may be a novel approach for some. You might want to demonstrate by giving your choices first.

Read out the questions one at a time, with the possible answers and get the group to discuss their responses in twos or threes.

1 What colour would you use to describe your way of life?

a red – stressed
b grey – under a permanent cloud
c blue – sad at the moment
d green – optimistic
e yellow – sunny and bright
f purple – intense

There could be other alternatives, including a striped combination of colours!

2 If you compared your way of life to a meal, what would it be? Why?

a fish and chips
b peaches and cream
c roast beef and Yorkshire pudding
d a fresh green salad
e a too-hot-to-handle curry

f stale cheese sandwich

g other _____

3 If you compared your way of life to a texture, what would it be? Why?

a sheepskin rug

b rock

c jelly

d thorny bush

e polished wooden shelf

f slushy snow

g other _____

BIBLE READING
I Peter 1:13–25

RELATIONAL BIBLE STUDY

IN DEPTH

MY STORY

GOING FURTHER

Things to remember ...

notes on the Bible verses

   I Peter 1:13–25

To live a Christ-like lifestyle does not mean that we need to become Jews, or even that we need to live without the comfort of a home and possessions of our own. This passage describes the 'inner' lifestyle of Jesus, and it is that which we must copy, irrespective of what outward lifestyle he may call us to.

1:13 The renewed life of the disciple needs the active involvement of the mind – thinking through, working out, reflecting on all the issues involved in living the new life.

1:17 The fear we are to have for God involves a respect that doesn't allow us to think lightly of his holiness and power.

1:22 Peter talks of a close link between personal holiness and obligations to the Christian community. The believer is not only born into a new relationship with God, but a new relationship with other Christians.

CHRIST-LIKE LIVING

BIBLE READING
1 Peter 1:13–25

RELATIONAL BIBLE STUDY

1 To be holy (1:15) means … (circle the most appropriate)

a going to church regularly.

b being a stick-in-the-mud.

c not swearing.

d living a morally upright life.

e loving God and other people.

f learning Bible verses by heart.

g dressing in white and pastel colours.

h being persecuted.

i being set apart to do God's work.

j other _____

IN DEPTH

1 How can we have our minds *prepared for action* (1:13)?

a praying

b spending our time only with Christians

c being sensitive to people's needs

d being aware of social issues

e having an enquiring mind

f obeying God

g other _____

2 What does it mean to live our lives in *reverent fear* (1:17). Tick the items that contribute to this, put a cross against those that don't, and a question mark when you aren't sure.

– trembling every time God's name is mentioned

– respecting creation

– working for justice

– being someone who is respected

– being humble

– living like a monk

– serving others

– taking hardship without complaint

– letting God having control

3 Christ sacrificed everything for us. What and when do you think we should give up when we are following him? Tick one column for each item.

	always	sometimes	never
fame			
money			
job			
home			
family			
social status			
time			
ambition			

MY STORY

1 How does the idea of living a holy life (1:15) sound to you?

a boring   **e** worthwhile
b exciting   **f** pointless
c difficult   **g** risky
d impossible   **h** other _____

2 How much of these areas of your life would you describe as 'holy' in the sense of being controlled by God? Fill in the circles like pie charts.

my thoughts   my money   my time

my speech   my leisure   my job

my emotions   my home life   my relationships

going further

1 In the Bible God's holiness is talked about in at least two different ways: meaning the complete 'otherness' of God from us, and meaning the complete moral perfection of God.

Have a look at these passages and summarise what they teach about the holiness of God:
Exodus 15:11

Psalm 99:1–5
Matthew 5:48
Psalm 5:4
Isaiah 6:1–5

2 Every Christian should aim for a holy life – set apart by God to be used when, where and how he chooses. This process is a matter of co-operation between the believer and the Holy Spirit. In Colossians, Paul describes this process in terms of putting off the old self and putting on the new self.

Read Colossians 3:5–17:

a What attitudes are Christians to get rid of?
b What attitudes are Christians to clothe themselves with?
c What is God's part in this process?

BRICKS IN THE WALL

AIM: To see that it is an honour and a responsibility for Christians to be actively involved in the life of the church.

NOTES FOR LEADERS

PRAYER/WORSHIP IDEAS

Opening prayer
A helpful theme for the opening prayer would be that of thankfulness for the local church.

Songs and hymns
Choose songs which refer to our co-dependence and to the theme of building up the church. Examples could include:

As we are gathered
Bind us together
I love you with the love of the Lord
I will give thanks to thee, O Lord, among the people
Jesus, how lovely you are
Let there be love shared among us
These are the days of Elijah

During the meeting
Give each person two or three Lego bricks. After they say a one-sentence prayer for a named member of the group of congregation, they should put the brick in the centre of the group, with each brick that's added being built into a small wall.

Closing prayer
Praise and thank God for the diversity of gifts represented in the group and in the church of which the group is a part.

ICEBREAKER
This drawing of a house shows a variety of bricks.

Ask people to choose what kind of brick they think they are, and then to share reasons for their choice. If the group knows each other well they might like to guess first what choice an individual has made.

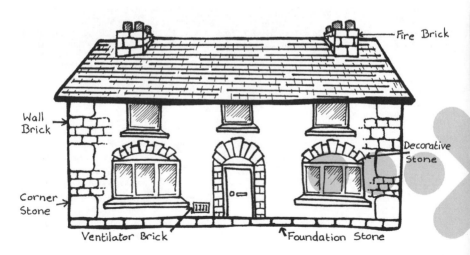

foundation stone	– reliable, strong, giving support to others, not always obvious.
fire brick	– resistant, able to withstand extreme conditions and survive strain
ventilator brick	– light and airy, allowing fresh air to come into the building
decorative stone	– adding to other people's enjoyment of life
corner stone	– in a strategic situation doing an important job
wall brick	– one of many fitting together to make up the whole, not standing out but important to overall strength and unity

BIBLE READING
1 Peter 2:4–10

RELATIONAL BIBLE STUDY

IN DEPTH
It may be helpful to explain to the group what a spiritual sacrifice is (see notes).

MY STORY

GOING FURTHER

notes on the Bible verses

 1 Peter 2:4–10

2:4 In the Old Testament, God is frequently described as a rock, giving security and salvation to his people – see, for example, Deuteronomy 32:15, 1 Samuel 2:2, Psalm 18:2. Here Peter applies this symbol to Jesus, making an implicit statement about his deity and his uniqueness. Jesus is a *living* stone not only because he is a person, but because he has been raised from the dead and will never die again.

2:5–8 The temple in Jerusalem was the focal point of Old Testament worship. Jesus had spoken of himself as the true temple (John 2:19–22), the only 'place' where God could be worshipped, the only person through whom God could be approached. The concept of sacrifice was a picture of what God was going to do through Jesus. And now that this reality

had arrived, many people preferred to hang on to the picture instead of experiencing the real thing, so rejecting Christ. Those who accepted him would be living stones, built into a new spiritual temple. And whereas in the Old Testament days only certain men could be priests and have access to God on the strength of the blood of slaughtered animals, now all can have access to God because of the blood of Jesus. Instead of animal sacrifices, the Christian can offer himself as a living sacrifice.

2:10 God rescued the Israelites from slavery in Egypt, making them his special nation, by covenant agreement. When they broke the terms of that agreement they suffered exile as a result; but when they repented, God built them up again as a nation. Now it's possible for all people to experience freedom from the slavery of sin in a new covenant with Jesus. And those who do so are part of his chosen people, the church.

BRICKS IN THE WALL

BIBLE READING
I Peter 2:4–10

RELATIONAL BIBLE STUDY

I Tick T for true and F for false. Peter described Jesus as the *living stone*. Using that image, would you say Christians are people who …

	T	F
a chisel the stone into a shape to suit themselves.	—	—
b build their lives on the stone.	—	—
c hide behind the stone.	—	—
d use the stone as the base for their own schemes.	—	—
e use the stone as a weapon against others.	—	—

2 The church is…	T	F
a a special building.	—	—
b a religious organisation.	—	—
c people who love Jesus Christ.	—	—
d a hymn-singing club.	—	—
e an employment agency for vicars.	—	—
f for weddings, baptisms and funerals.	—	—
g a place to pray.	—	—
h where God lives.	—	—
i other _____		

3 The church exists to…	T	F
a shelter us from problems.	—	—
b offer praise to God.	—	—
c provide organists with work.	—	—
d run jumble sales.	—	—
e fit people into a mould.	—	—
f provide a social club.	—	—
g help those in need, especially the poor.	—	—
h share the good news about Jesus.	—	—
i other _____		

IN DEPTH

I What do you think Peter means by *spiritual sacrifices acceptable to God (2:5)*?

_____

_____

2 How does Peter describe the Christian community?

Find three words or phrases in 2:5 _____

_____

_____

Find four words or phrases in 2:9

_____

_____

_____

_____

3 Peter says we are chosen so that we may *declare the praises* of God (2:9). What does that mean and how can we do it?

a individually _____

b together _____

MY STORY

1 In terms of a picture of you being built into a spiritual house, what stage is the building at now? Put a cross on the lines somewhere between the two extremes.

planning _____ demolition

laying foundations _____ roof completed

outer structure complete _____ internal decor complete

2 Share two causes for praising God in your own life. (Look back to 2:9.)

3 The temple in Jerusalem was a centre of worship. What do you, personally, expect …

a to contribute to the worship of the church? _____

_____

b to receive from the worship of the church? _____

_____

going further ∿∿

1 In the Old Testament only certain individuals were allowed to become priests (see Genesis 8:20; 31:54 and Exodus 28). The main functions of the priests were to offer sacrifices to God and to act as go-betweens between God and his people. By his death and resurrection, Jesus, *the great High Priest*, has abolished that old system. Look up these references about Jesus and compare them to the Old Testament verses.

Offering sacrifice:
Romans 3:25
Hebrews 7:23–28
Hebrews 10:1–10
1 Corinthians 5:7

Acting as go-between:
John 14:6
Colossians 1:20
1 Timothy 2:5
Hebrews 4:14–16

Ephesians 1:7
Ephesians 2:13
Revelation 1:5
Revelation 5:9
Colossians 1:20
1 Peter 1:18,19

Hebrews 7:23–27
Hebrews 9:13–15

2 On account of their faith in Christ, Christians have direct access to God and need no human mediators (see 1 Timothy 2:5 and 1 Peter 2:9–10). With this privilege there is also the responsibility to live as God's people in the world. How can Christians today act as priests/go-betweens/bridge builders between God and people?

SALT OF THE EARTH

AIM: To show that Christians are called to be useful and responsible citizens.

NOTES FOR LEADERS

PRAYER/ WORSHIP IDEAS

Opening prayer
Slowly read Luke 4:16–19, having suggested that while you do so, members of the group should pray silently for any people they know who are working with the poor, underprivileged, orphaned, widowed, displaced, sick, disabled, and prisoners.

Songs and hymns
Any songs which emphasise God's mission to his church and the need for the members of the Body of Christ to work together would be suitable, including:

A new commandment I give unto you
An army of ordinary people
For I'm building a people of power
Great is the darkness
Here I am, wholly available
Jesus, stand among us
Jesus, we enthrone you
Restore, O Lord, the honour of your name

During the meeting
Ask each person to sketch an outline on a piece of paper which symbolises one of the needy social areas of the local community, eg a bottle to represent problems with alcoholism, a coffin to represent the needs of the newly-bereaved and widowed, a credit card to represent the needs of those who are struggling with debt. Then, in threes or fours, share those concerns and pray briefly about them.

Closing prayer
Take up any specific concerns that have been discussed in the meeting along with expressing confidence in God as a champion of the needy.

ICEBREAKER
Before the meeting, prepare three large pieces of card, one with the word AGREE, one with DISAGREE and the third with DON'T KNOW written on them in letters large enough to read across the room, and put them up in prominent places around the room. Every time you read out a statement, group members should vote by moving to stand with one of the three cards depending on whether they agree, disagree, or don't know. Then you ask someone from the AGREE group to speak for two minutes in defence of the statement, and someone from the DON'T AGREE group to speak for two minutes against the statement. After that you read the statement again, and people can choose to change their position if they want to.

How many statements you use will depend on how much time you are able to allocate to this part of the meeting. Here are some suggestions, but you may well think of others which are contemporary hot issues.

- The safety belt law is an infringement of an individual's freedom and should be repealed.
- All advertising of alcohol should be banned.
- Rail fares should be massively subsidised by the government.
- People over 60 should not be allowed to drive unless they pass a special driving test.
- The terminally ill should be given assisted suicide if they want it.

BIBLE READING
1 Peter 2:11–17

RELATIONAL BIBLE STUDY
Your might want to draw people's attention to the fact that the Roman Empire was governed on authoritarian lines – that is, the people were expected to obey the dictates of the emperor without question. Britain is a democracy – government of the people, for the people, by the people. However, the basic principles of Peter's teaching apply to Christians in every kind of society.

IN DEPTH

MY STORY

GOING FURTHER

Things to remember ...

notes on the Bible verses

1 Peter 2:11–17

2:11 God's people should not feel at home in the society in which they live. Its standards, values and structures are alien to those of God. Peter sees them as foreigners in a hostile land. By *sinful desires*, he means those desires which are selfish and against God's will. The Christian is at war with these desires but is equipped by God to overcome them.

2:12 Christ said that his disciples were to be to the world what light is to darkness and what salt is to meat. So their lives illumine what God's love and mercy is doing and preserve against moral corruption. By *the day he visits us,*

Peter may have in mind the time of Christ's return, or he may have been thinking of a particular outpouring of God's mercy rather than his judgement.

2:13,14 These verses teach that the state authorities are the agents of God to maintain law and order. Christians should pray for those in authority. Sometimes, though, it is necessary to disobey the authorities in order to obey God (see Acts 5:29). The early Christians lived under authoritarian rule. There is a sense in which contemporary Christians living in democracies have an even greater responsibility towards it. Having brought it to office through the electoral processes, they should keep its laws, and encourage the godly exercise of power.

SALT OF THE EARTH

READING
I Peter 2:11–17

RELATIONAL BIBLE STUDY
I Tick A for ALWAYS, S for SOMETIMES and N for NEVER:

a As citizens, Christians should…   A   S   N

be well behaved.
obey the laws of the land.
respect other people's rights.
convert everybody.
expect everybody to conform to Christian moral standards.
vote Conservative.

b Submitting to every human authority means…   A   S   N

unquestioning obedience.
getting involved in local government.
starting a revolution.
working for changes where you believe they are needed.
being a doormat for God.

c Living as free people means doing…   A   S   N

exactly what you want, when you want, how you want.
exactly what you want when no one else is looking.
things that are in line with loving God and other people.
what your church says is OK.
what you feel is right.
what other people do.

d Respecting people means…   A   S   N

liking them.
wanting the best for them.
wanting them to believe what you believe.
leaving them to live their own lives.
treating them as individuals.
agreeing with them.
letting them have their own point of view.

IN DEPTH

I List five ways in which you, as a Christian, can 'do good' (2:12) in your society today.

a _____ d _____

b _____ e _____

c _____

2 List five groups of people who you feel are not respected (2:17) in your society today.

a _____   **d** _____
b _____   **e** _____
c _____

3 To fear God (2:17) means to remember who God is and stand in awe of him. List five ways in which you can demonstrate the fear of the Lord (eg proper use of his creation).

a _____   **d** _____
b _____   **e** _____
c _____

MY STORY

1 What benefits do you most appreciate as a citizen? Mark a cross at appropriate points on the lines.

a freedom of speech   a lot _____ not much
b health care   a lot _____ not much
c law and order   a lot _____ not much
d education   a lot _____ not much
e state benefits (financial) a lot _____ not much
f freedom of movement   a lot _____ not much
g other   a lot _____ not much

Share your responses and discuss within the group.

2 List any ways in which you take part in the life of your local community – anything from local council committees through to volunteering to help with reading in a primary school classroom.

_____
_____

going further

The New Testament teaches that governments are appointed by God and exist to maintain law and order. But at times it is obvious that ruling powers are opposing God's standards of love, justice, mercy, fair dealing etc. In such circumstances the Christian must obey God rather than the government. The story of Daniel is an example of this principle.

Read Daniel Chapter 6 and discuss the following questions:

a How could Daniel justify serving as a government official under a pagan ruler?
b What particular values did Daniel bring into his political work? How much are these qualities needed today?

c Why do you think Daniel met with opposition and how did he respond?
d Can you think of any circumstances in which you would feel compelled not to observe one of your country's laws?
e Daniel was delivered. Should Christians expect to be delivered from difficult situations today? (See also Daniel 3:17,18.)

STAND UP AND BE COUNTED

AIM: To show that God calls us to witness to our faith in deeds and words and to be prepared for the difficulties which may result.

NOTES FOR LEADERS

PRAYER/WORSHIP IDEAS

Opening prayer
This session will look at witnessing – often a sensitive subject. Pray that the Holy Spirit will give the group increased love for each other, and facilitate honesty and an openness to learn.

Songs and hymns
Choose songs which reflect the challenge of sharing the Good News and remind everyone that the work is really God's. These might include:

Fight the good fight with all thy might
For this purpose Christ was revealed
In heavenly love abiding
Jesus, lover of my soul, all-consuming fire is in your gaze
Praise God for the body
Rejoice, the Lord is King!
Shout for joy and sing, let your praises ring
Stand up, stand up for Jesus

During the meeting
Ask everyone to summarise in one sentence *the hope* that they have that they would want to share with others. Then ask each one to pray silently for another person, asking God to given them the opportunity to share their hope with them.

Closing prayer
Take the feedback from Question 4 of My Story and use that for a prayer of thanks and a prayer for growth.

ICEBREAKER
This icebreaker is optional, but if you include it you will need to allow at least 15 minutes. Explain that the point of the exercise is that we need to be disciplined in the way we act and speak, both being forms of witness for Christ.

The challenge of this icebreaker is being able to cope with one, simple responsibility. Each person is given five buttons or dried peas. For five minutes the group moves around asking each other questions. The only responsibility each member has is to avoid using the words 'yes' or 'no'. If either word is used, a button or dried pea is handed over to the one who cause the response. See who has the most buttons or dried peas at the end.

BIBLE READING
1 Peter 3:8–18

RELATIONAL BIBLE STUDY

IN DEPTH

MY STORY

GOING FURTHER

Things to remember ...

notes on the Bible verses

1 Peter 3:8–18

This passage highlights the two elements of witnessing – through actions (particularly the life of Christians together), and through words. Peter addresses the fact that witnessing will lead to suffering, and points his readers to Christ, whose obedience to God and consequent suffering brought us such good.

3:15 'Jesus is Lord' was probably the earliest Christian creed and confession (see 1 Corinthians 12:3; Romans 10:9; Philippians 2:11). To acknowledge the lordship of Christ is to submit to him totally, receiving the blessings he offers and accepting the responsibilities he commands. The *hope* that Peter mentions is not vague, wishful thinking in this context. It is a certainty that in the end God will triumph over evil (see Colossians 1:3–5) and that, for the Christian, death is a glorious new beginning.

STAND UP AND BE COUNTED

READING
1 Peter 3:8–18

RELATIONAL BIBLE STUDY

1 Circle the attitudes that Peter says Christians should adopt:

loving   hopeful   cheerful

     good   forceful

proud   humble   mean

     kind   truthful

guilty   peaceful   angry

     fearful   gentle

2 How can we *set apart Christ as Lord* (3:15)? Circle appropriate answers.

    love him   fear him

obey him   trust him

    talk to him   test him

be straight with him   keep quiet about him

worship him   debate him

complain to him   tell others about him

3 Why did Jesus die (3:18)?

a To give us something to tell others about.
b To lead us to God.
c As an example to his followers.
d To reveal God's power.
e As an act of humility.
f Because he couldn't save himself.
g Because he was a threat to the Roman authorities.
h other _____

IN DEPTH

1 Living in harmony (3:8) means…

a joining the church choir.
b living together in one large house.
c accepting people's differences.
d encouraging everyone to agree.
e being 'wishy-washy'.
f being prepared to listen.
g being prepared to change.
h other _____

2 When Christians are hurt by other people they should…

a give as good as they get.
b shrug it off.
c forgive.
d do something positive for the person who hurt them.
e find someone to talk to about it.
f pray.
g file the experience away inside as future ammunition.
h other _____

3 Giving *the reason for the hope that you have* (3:15) means

a taking people to your church.
b being a cheerful person in all circumstances.
c distributing tracts.
d telling your own experience of Jesus.
e becoming a missionary.
f bashing people over the head with the Bible.
g other _____

MY STORY

1 When I think of telling other people about Jesus I ...

a grab the first opportunity.
b cry, 'Help Lord! Show me how!'
c run a mile.
d feel terribly inadequate.
e remember that it's the job of ministers and preachers only.
f find an excuse, because they probably won't want to know.
g worry they will laugh at me.
h wait for a good time and place to do it.
I other _____

2 A time when I suffered because of my faith as a Christian was ...

_____

3 A time when I was able to speak for Jesus Christ was ...

_____

4 This group should, even in its meeting together, be a witness to Jesus. What are the characteristics of your group that would attract others? Tick the things you think they would find.

___ unity of purpose
___ sympathetic listening to each other
___ genuine love and concern for one another
___ willingness to spend time regularly to meet and learn
___ ability to accommodate differences of opinion
___ eagerness to do good

going further

1 What do the following Bible verses teach about witnessing with words?

I Corinthians 2:1,5
I Corinthians 13:1
Proverbs 14:5
Matthew 10:32

2 What do these verses teach about witnessing by actions?

Matthew 5:13–16
Matthew 7:21–23
James 2:14–19
I John 3:16–18

USE YOUR GIFTS

AIM: To show the need for Christians to work together in preparation for Christ's return.

NOTES FOR LEADERS

PRAYER/ WORSHIP IDEAS

Opening prayer
Ask the group to spend three minutes writing a one-sentence prayer which reflects thanks to God for something new they have learned to appreciate about him over the course of the BODYBUILDERS meetings.

Songs and hymns
Songs that encourage believers to follow the pattern set by Jesus and to look to his return would be appropriate. These could include:

Be thou my vision
Breathe on me, Breath of God
Fill thou my life, O Lord my God
From heaven you came
Hold me Lord, in your arms
I will offer up my life in spirit and truth
Master, speak! Thy servant heareth
O Jesus, I have promised
The King is among us
The Lord has led forth
We are here to praise you

During the meeting
Have a few minutes' discussion on the future of the group. Are there plans to meet again? How are people going to keep in touch? Pray about these plans.

Closing prayer
Pray for each other by name, using the words of Philippians 1:6.

ICE BREAKER
Two people are chosen, one as a shepherd and one as a sheep. (You might want to give the shepherd a few days' notice of this, so that he can prepare.) The sheep closes his eyes while the shepherd leads him around the room on an imaginary journey for about five minutes. The shepherd describes the route, scenery, weather conditions, animals, flowers, trees, other people, smells, etc as vividly as he can. Then the sheep opens his eyes and describes his feelings as he was being led. The group discusses the impact of the shepherd's 'travelogue' on the sheep's experience.

BIBLE READING
1 Peter 4:7 – 5:7

RELATIONAL BIBLE STUDY

IN DEPTH

MY STORY
Your knowledge of the group will help you decide how much sharing of these answers would be appropriate.

GOING FURTHER

Things I've learned leading this group ...

N.B. Which Bodybuilders title shall I use next?

notes on the Bible verses

 I Peter 4:7 – 5:7

It may be that the apostles thought that the return of Jesus was only a few years away. Certainly for us in the twenty-first century it remains true that our own earthly lifespan is not only short but can be prematurely ended without warning. Living in the shadow of eternity should focus our minds on the things of true importance.

4:9 Hospitality was seen as a Christian duty and a way of serving God. It was vital to the early church that its members were hospitable. Travelling missionaries and teachers needed somewhere to stay, and the church fellowship group met in homes.

4:10 Every Christian is given a gift from God (see I Corinthians 12, especially verse 7). Some gifts may not be easily recognised and may need to be 'discovered'. As well as special spiritual gifts, every material possession and personal quality we have is a gift from God and should be used in his service. Gifts are given to build up the Christian fellowship and make it effective in fulfilling God's purposes (see Ephesians 4:7,11–16).

5:1 Eldership was the basic office in the early church, and elders were alternatively called 'bishops' or 'overseers' and 'pastors' or 'shepherds'. Their responsibilities were varied, from leading, preaching and teaching through to managing finances.

5:2 The shepherd picture carries with it the idea of gentleness, caring, protecting, leading, wisdom etc. When Peter wrote this, he was almost certainly thinking of the time when Jesus entrusted him with this task (John 21:15–17).

USE YOUR GIFTS

BIBLE READING
I Peter 4:7 – 5:7

RELATIONAL BIBLE STUDY
I What sort of feelings does this passage give you?

a Panic – Jesus could return tomorrow.
b Concern – our church hasn't really got it together yet.
c Joy – one day this struggle to live a holy life will be over.
d Hope – we're going to really work at this, together.
e Puzzled – what have I got to offer?
f other _____

2 What do you understand by the word *gift* as used here?

a natural talents/flair
b learned skills
c secret instructions given by God to each Christian
d special abilities given by God to each Christian
e preaching
f other _____

3 If someone asked you how you were looking after the gift God had given you, how would you reply?

a What gift?
b If only I had time!
c Where can I go for training?
d I wish people would let me use it.
e That my business, it's private.
f I'm doing my best.
g other _____

IN DEPTH
I On the chart, I = 'this doesn't motivate me much at all' and 10 = 'this *really* motivates me!' Circle a number for each item.

My motives for serving God are ...

a to impress people.	1 2 3 4 5 6 7 8 9 10
b to please my family.	1 2 3 4 5 6 7 8 9 10
c to obey God.	1 2 3 4 5 6 7 8 9 10
d to find personal fulfilment.	1 2 3 4 5 6 7 8 9 10
e to spend my time usefully.	1 2 3 4 5 6 7 8 9 10
f to do what the church teaches.	1 2 3 4 5 6 7 8 9 10
g other _____	1 2 3 4 5 6 7 8 9 10

2 What have I done to develop the gifts God has given me? Circle an answer for each possibility.

a gone on a training course	yes	no
b prayed about them	yes	no
c practised them	yes	no
d read books on the subject	yes	no
e read the Bible for help	yes	no
f learned from the example of others	yes	no
g other _____		

MY STORY

1 Think about someone who has been a 'shepherd' to you in the past (5:2,3). How did he or she guide you?

_____

_____

2 In what areas of your life do you feel in need of a 'shepherd' now?

a your relationships   **e** your future

b your work   **f** your relationship with God

c your finances   **g** your prayer life

d your place in the church   **h** other _____

3 Look at this list of gifts/talents/skills. Are there any of them against which you would like to put your name? Put a 'Y' if you are already using this gift in your local church or group, and a 'P' if it's area you'd like to pray about and perhaps use in the future.

teaching ____	counselling ____	encouraging ____
catering ____	serving ____	organising ____
listening ____	youth work ____	children's work ____
prophesying ____	caring ____	praying ____
leading worship ____	preaching ____	wisdom ____
interpreting	healing ____	music ministry ____
peacemaking ____	leading ____	other _____

going further 〰️

Jesus said that the characteristic which would identify his disciples was love (John 13:34,35). Peter says we are to love each other *deeply* – *deeply* implies constant, intense, strenuous effort – because *love covers over a multitude of sins*.

Each of the following verses reflects a different aspect of love. As you read each one, think about
- what does this teach about love?
- how can this teaching be expressed in your life?

Matthew 5:43–48
Mark 12:28–31

Luke 10:25–37
John 13:34,35
Romans 12:9,10
1 Corinthians 13:1–13
Ephesians 4:2
2 Timothy 1:7
James 2:14–17
2 Peter 1:5–9
1 John 3:18
John 4:20,21

'Does your Bible study deal with the issues that friends are talking about at the pub or in the office?'

If you want to talk to your friends about why the Bible is relevant to what they are into, these are the Bible studies for you.
Mike Pilavachi, Soul Survivor

A great way to explore up-to-date issues and concerns in the light of the Bible.
Rev Dr Michael Green, Advisor in Evangelism to the Archbishops of Canterbury and York

How can you engage with friends and colleagues as they discuss best-selling novels, chart music, pop culture TV shows or Oscar-nominated films?

CONNECT can help – innovative, creative and thought-provoking Bible studies for groups available as an electronic download or in print.

Titles available

- Billy Elliot
- The Matrix
- Harry Potter
- TV Game Shows
- Chocolat
- How to be Good
- U2: All that you can't leave behind

With more coming soon

Available from all good Christian bookshops
from www.scriptureunion.org.uk
from Scripture Union Mail Order: PO Box 5148, Milton Keynes MLO, MK2 2YX
Tel 01908 856006
or as an electronic download from www.connectbiblestudies.com

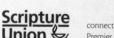

connect Bible Studies are jointly produced by Scripture Union, Premier Media Group and Damaris Trust.